T0125194

SUNS LEGENDS ALPHABET

Words by Robin Feiner

A is for **A**lvan Adams. This stalwart of the 1970s and '80s played his entire 13-year career with the Suns. Double A was a double-double machine. He holds franchise records for games, rebounds, and steals. His legendary 1975–76 Rookie of the Year and All-Star play helped Phoenix make its first Finals.

B is for Charles **B**arkley. One of the game's greatest characters, Barkley's play also did plenty of talking. An All-Star Suns player from 1992–96, his legendary mix of scoring, passing, and rebounding made him an all-time great power forward. Chuck led Phoenix to the Finals in his 1992–93 MVP season.

**C is for Chris Paul.
Top-three all-time in NBA
career assists, Suns fans
quickly praised The Point
God after his 2020 arrival.
CP3 helped transform a young
team with his legendary
leadership, helping Phoenix
break a 10-year playoff
drought and taking the
franchise to within two
wins of the title.**

D is for Devin Booker. This superstar two-guard quickly grew into one of the game's elite scorers. In his second season in 2017, Book became just the sixth player to drop 70 points in a game. His sweet shooting was a huge part of the Suns' 2021 Finals run.

E is for **E**ddie Johnson. The 1988–89 Sixth Man of the Year, Johnson provided vital bench scoring for the Suns. But he's perhaps even better known in Phoenix as a broadcasting legend. Johnson has shared his passion for the city and team on TV and radio for over 20 years.

F is for Cotton **F**itzsimmons. A master motivator, this legend had a .621 winning percentage in his seven full seasons coaching the Suns and was the 1988–89 Coach of the Year. Fitzsimmons helped guide Phoenix through some of the team's darkest days from the bench, the front office, and the broadcasting booth.

G is for Goran Dragic. Dragic's ball handling and scoring helped lighten Steve Nash's load during the legendary 7 Seconds or Less era. The Dragon was in full flight in the 2010 playoffs, catching fire to score 23 fourth-quarter points against the rival San Antonio Spurs in the second round.

H is for Connie **H**awkins. An All-Star in his four full Phoenix seasons, many never saw Hawkins' full array of legendary skills. Considered maybe the most talented forward of his generation by his peers, this high-flying Hall of Famer blew by defenders on his way to the rim.

I is for Matt Ishbia.
The man who led the Suns
out of the dark final days
of Robert Sarver's ownership.
Ishbia didn't wait to make a
legendary splash, trading for
superstar Kevin Durant within
days of officially taking over
the team in a win-now move
that excited fans.

Jj

J is for Kevin Johnson.
The Suns made the playoffs
every season from 1989–2000.
KJ's playmaking and scoring
were a big reason why. He
retired leading the franchise
in assists and provided plenty
of memorable moments –
including his poster of
Hakeem Olajuwon in the
1994 playoffs – before
injuries caught up to him
and forced his retirement.

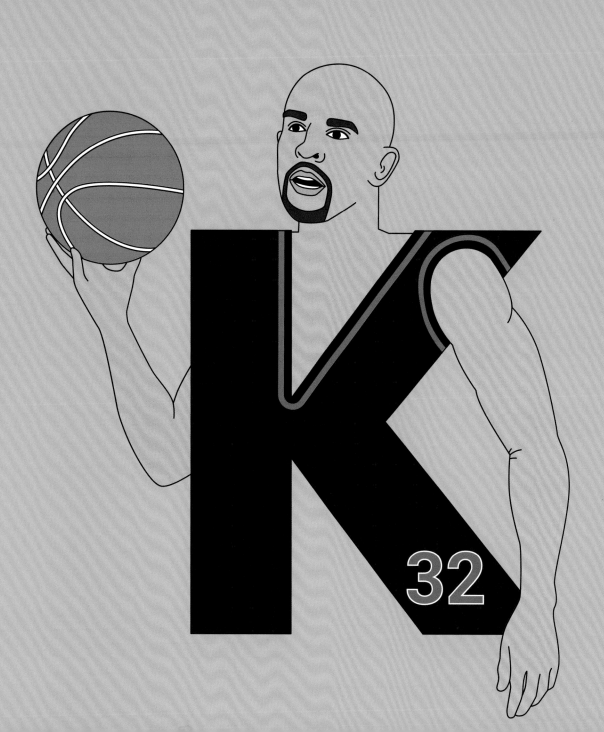

K is for Jason **K**idd.
Kidd's legendary court vision and bag full of passes helped him lead the league in assists the final three of his four full seasons with the suns from 1997–2001. J-Kidd was also a bulldog defender, great rebounding guard, and solid scorer, earning three All-Star appearances with the Suns.

Ll

L is for Tom Leander.
From ballboy to broadcaster,
this legend has delivered
the Suns to viewers and
listeners for more than 25
years. Whether dropping
his legendary 'Elevate and
detonate!' catchphrase
after a massive dunk or
delivering pre-game or post-
game analysis, Leander
is a mainstay on TV for
generations of fans.

M is for **M**ike D'Antoni. His legendary 7 Seconds or Less style made Phoenix one of the most exciting teams ever. The 2004–05 Coach of the Year won tons of games. While injuries, suspensions, and outrageous officiating in the playoffs helped crush title hopes, D'Antoni's style changed the NBA.

N is for Steve **N**ash. The conductor of the 7 Seconds or Less Suns, Nash is arguably the greatest Sun ever. A sensational shooter and premier passer, Nash was a six-time All-Star, a back-to-back MVP, and a five-time league leader in assists.

O is for **O**liver Miller. The sun might've set early on Phoenix's 1993 Finals run if it weren't for this rookie center's legendary playoff heroics. With an increased role, Miller helped the Suns win three straight games to survive first-round elimination, including nine overtime points in the series-deciding Game 5.

P is for Paul Westphal. Westy had a brilliant basketball mind. His clever timeout idea helped extend the legendary 1976 Finals triple-overtime game. A potent scorer and four-time All-Star with Phoenix, Westphal then coached the Suns into an early 1990s Western Conference powerhouse.

Q is for **Q**uentin Richardson. Before becoming a Knucklehead podcaster, Q-Rich joined the legendary 7 Seconds or Less Suns for the 2004–05 season. With coach Mike D'Antoni's blessing, Richardson launched from long range, leading the league in attempts and tying for the most makes from beyond the arc.

**R is for Raja Bell.
Evolving into a three-
and-D master, Bell provided
toughness and selfless play
for the offensive-minded
7 Seconds or Less Suns.
Unafraid of battling the
league's best players, Bell's
2000s rivalry with Kobe
Bryant peaked with a
legendary clothesline in
the 2006 playoffs.**

S is for Amar'e **S**toudemire. Standing tall and talented, STAT played his first eight seasons in Phoenix from 2002–10. When healthy, Stoudemire earned five All-Star nods with the high-flying 7 Seconds or Less Suns. His legendary pick-and-roll connection with Steve Nash led to tons of buckets.

T is for **T**om Chambers. Chambers had a sweet shot despite being almost 7 feet tall. Forming a dynamic duo with guard Kevin Johnson, Chambers set a single-season franchise scoring record of 27.2 points per game in 1989–90. It included a legendary 60-point outburst against his former team Seattle.

U is for **U**ncle Cliffy.
One of the most legendary teammates in Suns history, Cliff Robinson provided strong scoring, defense, and lineup flexibility for four straight Phoenix playoff teams from 1997–2001. Almost always sporting his signature head-band, Robinson was known for playing with great energy.

V is for Dick **V**an Arsdale. This shooting guard was The Original Sun – the franchise's first player back in 1968. The Flying Dutchman, with his blend of youth and experience, scored the team's first NBA points and logged tons of minutes. His nine-year Suns career started with three All-Star appearances.

W is for **W**alter Davis. The 1977–78 Rookie of the Year's legendary, speedy style helped him average 24.2 points per game en route to his first of six All-Star Games. Perhaps Phoenix's greatest pure shooter, The Greyhound left the team in 1988 as its all-time leading scorer.

X is for The Matri**x**.
Shawn Marion's versatility helped unlock the potential of the 7 Seconds or Less Suns. Nicknamed The Matrix for his legendary athleticism, Marion could guard all five positions, was a strong rebounder, and scored from everywhere on the floor. He was a Swiss Army knife in basketball shoes.

Yy

Y is for Executive of the Year. Jerry Colangelo, the first general manager of the Suns, is the only person to win this award four times with one team. Entering as the youngest general manager in US professional sports, Colangelo oversaw many of the most legendary periods in Phoenix's history.

Z is for **Z**arko Cabarkapa. A legendary 'What if?' for Suns fans. In November 2003, this rookie was starting to flash some skill. But a dirty play broke his wrist, and he was never the same. Maybe he could've been the difference for the 2000s Suns teams that repeatedly came up short.

The ever-expanding legendary library

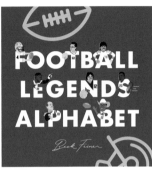

EXPLORE THESE LEGENDARY ALPHABETS & MORE AT WWW.ALPHABETLEGENDS.COM

SUNS LEGENDS ALPHABET
www.alphabetlegends.com

Published by Alphabet Legends Pty Ltd in 2023
Created by Beck Feiner
Copyright © Alphabet Legends Pty Ltd 2023

Printed and bound in China.

9780645851465

ALPHABET LEGENDS